Hot Rod

Written by
Stephen Rickard

Look at the cars parked in the warm sun.

The cars are all different, but they are all hot rods.

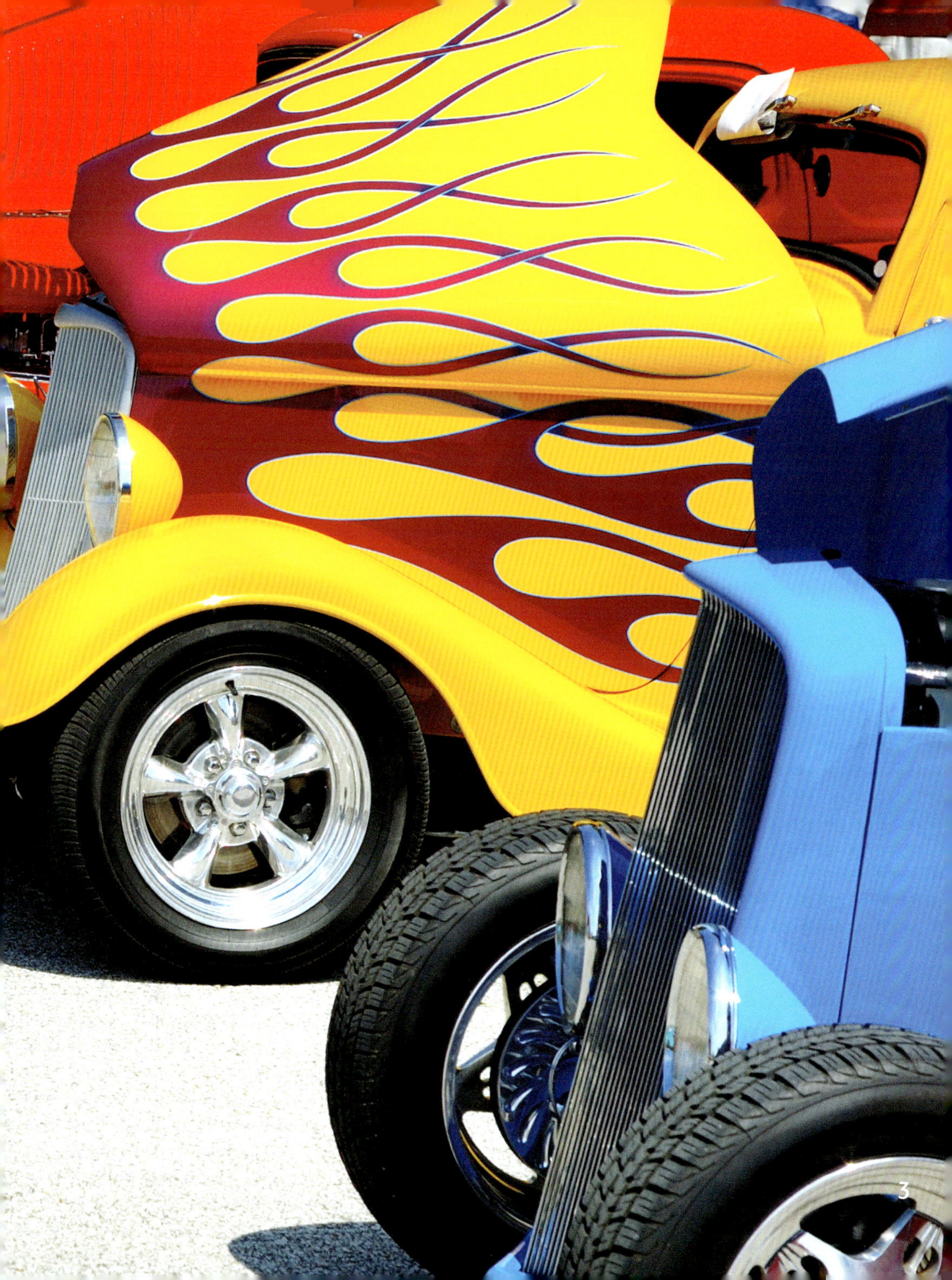

Hot rods started in the USA in the 1930s.

The cars were fixed to be quick. They all had extra power.

This hot rod is from a 1923 Ford T Bucket.

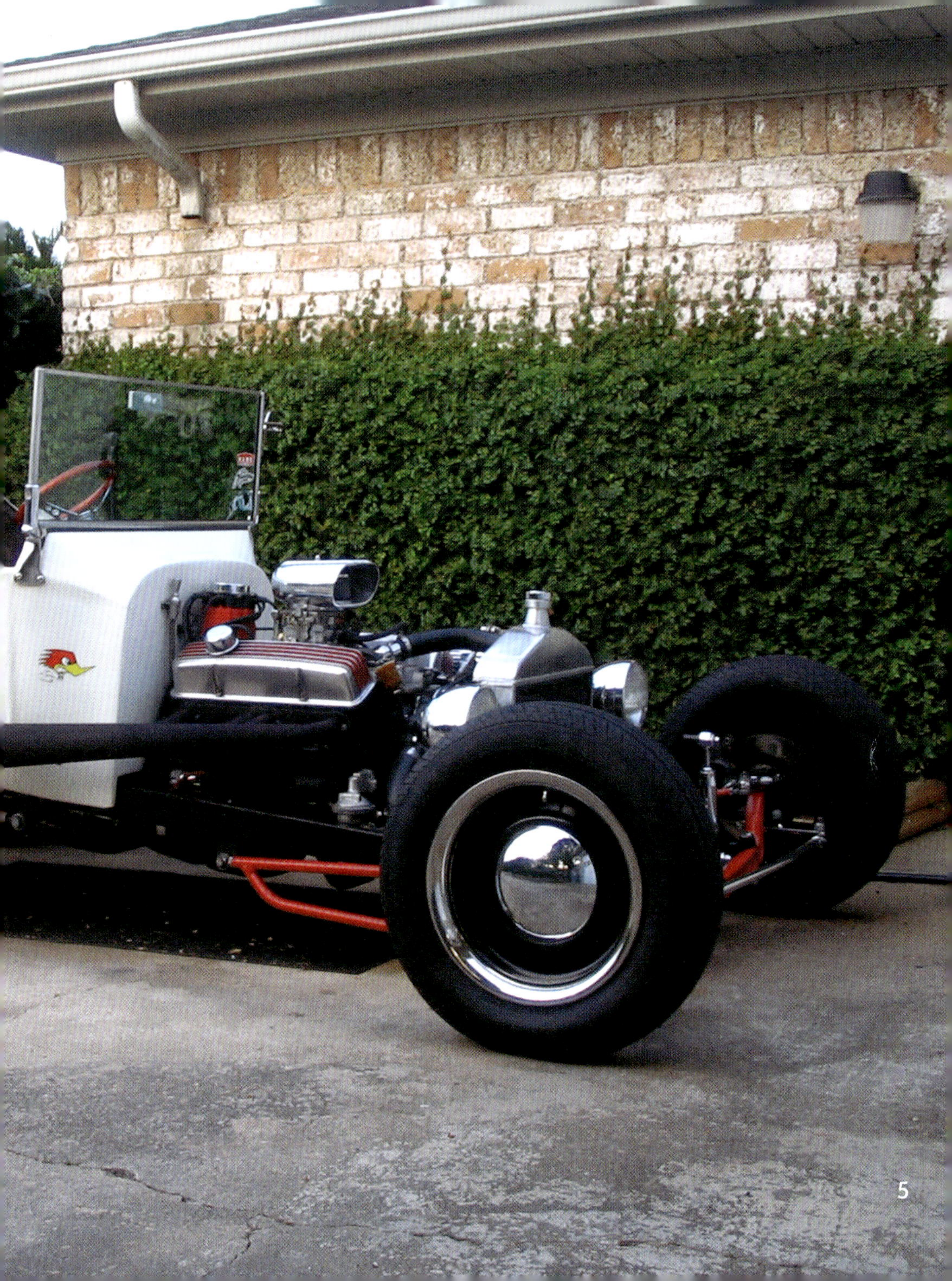

Hot rods look good.

They are low. Sometimes the top is cut down. You must be little to fit in the car!

The cars are bright, too.

Look at this hot rod. Is this a cool car?

It will give you a buzz to look at it and to travel in it.

This hot rod is not so bright.

In fact it is dull!

Rust is not as bright as red or green!

This is a **rat rod**. It is as fast as a hot rod, but it looks as if it is not finished.

Rat rods look cool, too!

Some hot rods are big.

Some hot rods are little.

Some hot rods are bright.

Some hot rods are dull.

All hot rods are quick and all hot rods give you a buzz!

11

You can hot rod a van or a truck.

This truck is now a rat rod.

12

In the 1960s, hot rods were seen in the streets. They were **street rods**.

Street rod cars were not as odd as hot rods.

13

Wait for the flag to drop, then . . . start!

Burn rubber and go!

Who will be the winner?

What sort of car will you get?

A hot rod, a rat rod or a street rod?